THE WHOLE MEGILLAH*

SHOSHANA SILBERMAN

ILLUSTRATED BY
KATHERINE JANUS KAHN

(*ALMOST)

KAR-BEN COPIES, INC.   ROCKVILLE, MD

DEDICATION

To my mother, Betty Ribner Borok, who like the Esther of the Megillah
faces life with courage and caring...
To my sons Steve and Gabe, for cheering me on...
To my daughter Lisa for writing the stage directions to the Purim play...
To my husband Mel for his continuous encouragement and support...
To the young and young at heart who have joyously celebrated Purim
with me at The Jewish Center...
  this Megillah is lovingly dedicated.

Bible. O.T. Esther, Hebrew. 1990.
  The Whole Megillah (Almost)/Shoshana Silberman; illustrated by Katherine
Janus Kahn.
    p.   cm.
  English and Hebrew.
  Summary: Includes abbreviated chapter summaries of the Book of Esther, com-
mentaries, a play script, and music and costume ideas.
  ISBN 0-929371-23-2
  1. Bible. O.T. Esther—Textbooks. 2. Purim—Juvenile literature. [1. Bible. O.T.
Esther. 2. Purim. 3. Hebrew language materials—Bilingual.] I. Silberman, Shoshana.
II. Kahn, Katherine, ill. III. Bible O.T. Esther. English. Silberman. 1990 IV. Title.
BS1372.S47   1990
296.4'36—dc20   90-5137
                                                                        CIP
                                                                       AC HE

INTRODUCTION

This Megillah is designed for congregations, schools, and families who prefer an abridged English version of the story, or wish to have a special Megillah reading geared to young children. Each chapter summary is accompanied by selected commentaries and questions to spark discussion about the text and its meaning for our day.

Hebrew verses with cantillation introduce each chapter. Songs, Purim trivia, and suggestions for making the reading more festive are included. We hope this version will lead older children and adults to study the "whole Megillah" with all its commentaries.

May all your Adars be happy.

◆ *Shoshana Silberman*

CONTENTS

ABOUT PURIM

Purim marks an event which supposedly happened in the fifth century B.C.E. in Susa, Persia. Scholars have long debated whether the Book of Esther is based on historical fact or is a masterpiece of fiction.

Those who consider the events to be history point to the countless details that reveal the author's knowledge of Persian life and letters. They also note that a Persian document mentions a government official named "Marduka" who resembles the Jewish hero, Mordechai. The Ahashuerus of the Purim story, they claim, is either Xerxes I or Artaxerxes II.

On the opposing side are those who believe that the Book of Esther is purely fiction. They point out that there is no reference to a Jewish queen in Persian historical records. According to Herodotus, the queen at the time was Amestris. Persia's queen needed to come from one of seven noble families. She was never chosen from a beauty contest! To further prove this thesis, scholars note that, unlike other books of the Bible, the name of God is not mentioned.

Some say Esther was written at the time of the Maccabean revolt (165 B.C.E.). At this moment of victory, the book might have been composed to reinforce the national mood of confidence. Others think that Purim co-opted popular pagan car-

nivals of the era. In particular, the Babylonians held a new year celebration when they believed their gods, Marduk and Ishtar, cast lots to determine each person's fate for the coming year. The elements of the festival were transformed into Purim, with Marduk becoming Mordechai and Ishtar becoming Esther.

◆◆◆◆◆◆◆◆◆◆◆◆◆◆◆◆◆◆◆◆◆◆◆◆◆◆◆◆

Why has a story whose historical basis is in question remained a Jewish "bestseller"? Although Purim may not have occurred in the time and place described in the Megillah, such events did, in fact, happen throughout Jewish history. Haman has become the symbol of evil and the embodiment of anti-Semitism in every land and in every country. The story of Purim has given hope that oppression against Jews will cease to exist. Telling the story has also helped us laugh at our plight. During the times when we have been a powerless minority living on foreign soil, humor became our potent weapon to combat anger and fear. The Megillah is a reminder of the need to be vigilant in the diaspora. It reinforces our commitment to work for and preserve human rights—our own and those of other people.

ADDING ZEST TO THE MEGILLAH READING

Make your Megillah reading special. Here are some ideas to get you started:

◆ Assign participants to pantomime the story as it is being read.

◆ Try a puppet show. Have children make large puppets to act out the reading. You may want to make hand puppets out of old socks, or create the faces of the characters on paper plates or posterboard and mount them on sticks.

◆ Create a "Gantze" (whole) Megillah. Have each class or youth group draw a mural of a different scene on a large roll of paper. The "Gantze Megillah" can be unrolled as the reading progresses.

◆ Have children make their own groggers in school or at home. Dried beans or coins are good fillers for decorated juice cans.

◆ Distribute Purim balloons to pop when Haman's name is mentioned.

◆ Invite each family to bring a plate of shalach manot (Purim goodies) to exchange with another family.

◆ To encourage adults and children to wear costumes, hold a Purim lottery ("Purim" *means* lottery). Draw names of those who come in costume, and award them prizes.

◆ Have a bag of extra hats and masks on hand for newcomers and those shy about coming in costume.

◆ Invite masqueraders to join in a gala Purim parade. Give everyone a certificate or small gift for participating.

◆ Conclude with a Purim Ball. Hire a band, or play recordings of klezmer music and have a *freilach* (festive) celebration.

BETWEEN CHAPTERS

- Sing Purim songs (some are included in this book), or invite participants to write original ones to familiar tunes.
- Have mini-parades. Give all the Esthers, hamantaschen, superheroes, and jesters a turn at showing off.
- Select a volunteer "talk show host" to interview important persons in the story, such as Vashti, Haman, and Esther, or even supporting characters, such as Bigtan and Teresh, or the King's horse.
- Assign "reporters" to cover parts of the story as they are happening. Get live coverage of the king's feast, the beauty contest, the king's sleepless night.

TZEDAKAH

- It is traditional to give half-dollars to tzedakah to commemorate the half-shekels the Jews gave to support the Holy Temple. Put out containers for organizations who help the needy, ill, or handicapped.
- Ask participants to bring canned goods and non-perishables to contribute to a food bank.
- Have each family bring a plate of shalach manot for a newcomer or senior citizen in the community.

BLESSINGS

BEFORE WE READ THE MEGILLAH,
WE SAY THREE BLESSINGS:

בָּרוּךְ אַתָּה, יְיָ אֱלֹהֵינוּ, מֶלֶךְ הָעוֹלָם, אֲשֶׁר קִדְּשָׁנוּ בְּמִצְוֹתָיו
וְצִוָּנוּ עַל מִקְרָא מְגִלָּה.

Baruch Atah Adonai Eloheinu melech ha'olam asher kid'shanu b'mitzvotav v'tzivanu al mikra Megillah.

We praise You, Adonai our God, Ruler of the Universe, Who has made us holy by Your mitzvot and commands us to read the Megillah.

בָּרוּךְ אַתָּה, יְיָ אֱלֹהֵינוּ, מֶלֶךְ הָעוֹלָם, שֶׁעָשָׂה נִסִּים לַאֲבוֹתֵינוּ
בַּיָּמִים הָהֵם בַּזְּמַן הַזֶּה.

Baruch Atah Adonai Eloheinu melech ha'olam she'asah nisim la'avoteinu bayamim hahem baz'man hazeh.

We praise You, Adonai our God, Ruler of the Universe, Who made miracles for our ancestors in those days.

בָּרוּךְ אַתָּה, יְיָ אֱלֹהֵינוּ, מֶלֶךְ הָעוֹלָם, שֶׁהֶחֱיָנוּ וְקִיְּמָנוּ
וְהִגִּיעָנוּ לַזְּמַן הַזֶּה.

Baruch Atah Adonai Eloheinu melech ha'olam shehecheyanu, v'kiy'manu v'higiyanu laz'man hazeh.

We praise You, Adonai our God, Ruler of the Universe, Who has kept us alive and well so that we can celebrate this special time.

וַיְהִי בִּימֵי אֲחַשְׁוֵרוֹשׁ הוּא אֲחַשְׁוֵרוֹשׁ
הַמֹּלֵךְ מֵהֹדוּ וְעַד־כּוּשׁ שֶׁבַע וְעֶשְׂרִים
וּמֵאָה מְדִינָה: בַּיָּמִים הָהֵם כְּשֶׁבֶת הַמֶּלֶךְ
אֲחַשְׁוֵרוֹשׁ עַל כִּסֵּא מַלְכוּתוֹ אֲשֶׁר
בְּשׁוּשַׁן הַבִּירָה: בִּשְׁנַת שָׁלוֹשׁ לְמָלְכוֹ
עָשָׂה מִשְׁתֶּה לְכָל־שָׂרָיו וַעֲבָדָיו חֵיל
פָּרַס וּמָדַי הַפַּרְתְּמִים וְשָׂרֵי הַמְּדִינוֹת
לְפָנָיו:

King Ahashuerus of Persia ruled over 127 provinces from India to Ethiopia. In the third year of his reign, he gave a sumptuous banquet for all his nobles and high officials. It lasted for 180 days!

Afterwards, the King held a week-long feast for all the people who lived in Shushan. Ahashuerus displayed the glorious riches of his kingdom, and served an unlimited amount of royal wine. At the same time, his Queen, Vashti, gave a banquet for the women of the palace.

On the seventh day of drinking and merrymaking, Ahashuerus ordered Queen Vashti to appear, so that his nobles might admire her beauty. But Vashti refused.

Ahashuerus was furious. He asked his advisors what should be done to Vashti for not obeying his command and humiliating him before his subjects. His advisor Memuchan suggested that Vashti be banished from the throne. This action would restore the King's honor and would be a warning to the other wives in the kingdom. And so it happened.

The rabbis portray Vashti as uncaring. They say she forced Jewish women to weave and spin on the Sabbath. Nowhere, however, does this portrayal of Vashti appear in the text. In fact, feminists think of her as a heroine. Many interpret her refusal to appear at the King's feast as an act of modesty.

Was Vashti wrong to refuse to obey the King's request, or was she a brave heroine?

Would you have obeyed the King if you were Vashti? Why or why not?

Why is it foolish to command someone to show you honor and respect?

Compare Vashti's plight with women in the Middle East today.

Ahashuerus is portrayed in the opening chapter as being powerful but not completely in control. When Memuchan convinces him to take revenge against Vashti, it is the first, but not the last time, that the King will do something foolish.

If you could pick only one word to describe Ahashuerus, what would it be?

Imagine you were a king or queen. What three things would you want for yourself and your subjects?

What problems did Ahashuerus's drinking cause him?

Do you think it is fair for a king to have great riches while some of his subjects live in poverty?

When and how have modern rulers lived an opulent life style that diminished their effectiveness as a leader?

אַחַר֩ הַדְּבָרִ֨ים הָאֵ֜לֶּה כְּשֹׁ֗ךְ חֲמַ֤ת הַמֶּ֙לֶךְ֙ אֲחַשְׁוֵרֹ֔ושׁ זָכַ֣ר אֶת־וַשְׁתִּ֔י וְאֵ֥ת אֲשֶׁר־עָשָׂ֖תָה וְאֵ֥ת אֲשֶׁר־נִגְזַ֥ר עָלֶֽיהָ: וַיֹּאמְר֥וּ נַעֲרֵֽי־הַמֶּ֖לֶךְ מְשָׁרְתָ֑יו יְבַקְשׁ֥וּ לַמֶּ֖לֶךְ נְעָר֥וֹת בְּתוּל֖וֹת טוֹב֥וֹת מַרְאֶֽה: וְיַפְקֵ֨ד הַמֶּ֜לֶךְ פְּקִידִ֗ים בְּכָל־מְדִינ֣וֹת מַלְכוּתֹ֔ו וְיִקְבְּצ֣וּ אֶת־כָּל־נַעֲרָה־בְתוּלָ֣ה טוֹבַ֣ת מַרְאֶ֡ה אֶל־שׁוּשַׁ֨ן הַבִּירָ֜ה אֶל־בֵּ֣ית הַנָּשִׁ֗ים אֶל־יַ֥ד הֵגֶ֛א סְרִ֥יס הַמֶּ֖לֶךְ שֹׁמֵ֣ר הַנָּשִׁ֑ים וְנָת֖וֹן תַּמְרֻקֵיהֶֽן:

When his anger subsided, Ahashuerus thought about what he had done and found that he missed Vashti. His advisors spoke out: "Let us organize a beauty contest among the maidens of the kingdom to choose a new queen." The King was pleased with this idea and agreed at once to the plan.

There was a Jew in Shushan named Mordechai, who was an official in the King's court. His cousin, whom he adopted, was among the beautiful maidens of Shushan brought to the palace for the contest. Her name was Esther, which in Hebrew is Hadassah.

Before they appeared before the King, the contestants spent months being pampered with cosmetics and oils. Only Esther appeared without perfumes or fancy jewels. Nonetheless, she won the King's heart, and he crowned her Queen of Persia. As Mordechai had instructed her, Esther did not reveal her background to Ahashuerus.

Soon thereafter, Mordechai overheard two servants, Bigthan and Teresh, plotting to kill the king. He told Esther, who reported it to Ahashuerus. The criminals were punished, and the deed was recorded in the King's record book.

What do the names Mordechai and Esther mean? Many scholars think the story is an adaptation of a Persian tale. Mordechai is Marduk, the god of Babylon, and Esther is the goddess Ishtar. The Talmud explains that as myrrh (mor) is the foremost of spices, so Mordechai was the most righteous in his generation. Esther's Hebrew name, Hadassah, means myrtle, a fragrant flower. Another midrash says the name Esther is from the word "nistar," which means hidden.

Why would Esther be called "hidden?"

Why did Mordechai ask Esther not to tell that she was Jewish? Would this be a hard secret to keep?

Did you ever not want to tell someone you were Jewish? How did you feel?

When else in history were Jews hidden?

In revealing the plot against the king's life, Mordechai got involved.

What do we risk when we get involved? What are the rewards?

It was certainly lucky that Mordechai overheard the plot to kill the king.

When else does chance or "mazal" play a role in the Purim story?

This is the second time Ahashuerus eagerly followed other people's advice.

How can this quality in a leader be a problem or even dangerous?

It is not clear from the text if Esther enters the contest voluntarily. Some view her as a martyr, persuaded to obey the king's request. Others say she was an assimilated Jew who seized the opportunity to become Queen.

Do you think Esther wanted to be in the beauty contest?

Hadassah, the Women's National Zionist Organization which was founded on Purim in 1912, was named after this Jewish heroine.

Here are some Megillah-reading customs:

- The Megillah is chanted to a special melody.

- It is a custom to unroll the Megillah and fold it over like a letter before reading it.

- The names of Haman's ten sons are read in one breath, because they were killed simultaneously.

- The four verses that refer to the redemption of the Jews are read in a louder voice or by the congregation.

- Some readers change voices as they read the parts of different characters in the story.

CHAG PURIM

Levin Kipnis
Folk Song

Chag Pu - rim chag Pu - rim chag ga - dol hu la - y'hu - dim
ma - se - chot ra'a - sha - nim z'mi - rot ri - ku - dim
ha - va nar - i - sha rash rash rash ha - va nar - i - sha rash rash rash
ha - va nar - i - sha rash rash rash ba - ra - a - sha - nim

Purim's here, Purim's here
Gayest day of all the year.
Mask your eyes in disguise,
Sing out loud and clear.

Chorus:
Hava narisha rash, rash, rash, (3)
Now that Purim's here.

אַחַר הַדְּבָרִים הָאֵלֶּה גִּדַּל הַמֶּלֶךְ אֲחַשְׁוֵרוֹשׁ אֶת־הָמָן בֶּן־הַמְּדָתָא הָאֲגָגִי וַיְנַשְּׂאֵהוּ וַיָּשֶׂם אֶת־כִּסְאוֹ מֵעַל כָּל־הַשָּׂרִים אֲשֶׁר אִתּוֹ: וְכָל־עַבְדֵי הַמֶּלֶךְ אֲשֶׁר־בְּשַׁעַר הַמֶּלֶךְ כֹּרְעִים וּמִשְׁתַּחֲוִים לְהָמָן כִּי־כֵן צִוָּה־לוֹ הַמֶּלֶךְ וּמָרְדֳּכַי לֹא יִכְרַע וְלֹא יִשְׁתַּחֲוֶה: וַיֹּאמְרוּ עַבְדֵי הַמֶּלֶךְ אֲשֶׁר־בְּשַׁעַר הַמֶּלֶךְ לְמָרְדֳּכָי מַדּוּעַ אַתָּה עוֹבֵר אֵת מִצְוַת הַמֶּלֶךְ:

Sometime afterwards, the King promoted HAMAN to the position of minister. All those in the palace court knelt and bowed before HAMAN, except for Mordechai who explained that he was a Jew. Angered by Mordechai's refusal, HAMAN plotted to destroy Mordechai, his family, and all the Jews in the kingdom.

HAMAN cast lots (Purim) to determine the day on which the Jews would die. That day turned out to be the 13th day of the month of Adar. HAMAN persuaded the King to go along with his evil plan by saying: "There is a certain people, scattered throughout the provinces of the kingdom, who have their own laws and customs. They are a threat to you." To further convince Ahashuerus, HAMAN offered to donate 10,000 silver coins to the royal treasury. The king believed HAMAN's lie. He issued a decree, sealed with the royal stamp, to kill the Jews - young and old, children and women - on the 13th day of Adar, and to keep all their possessions.

The custom of making noise at the mention of Haman's name, which appears for the first time in Chapter III, is based on the Torah commandment to "blot out the name of Amalek," the cruel enemy who attacked the Jewish people from behind as they left Egypt. (Exod. XVII: 8-16; Deut. XXV: 17-19.) Haman is said to be descended from Amalek. The most popular noisemaker is the grogger, based on a medieval musical instrument. In Yiddish, it is also called a *klapper* or *dreyer,* and in Hebrew, a *ra'ashan.* Groggers have been made from silver, bronze, and wood, and filled with beans, nails, or pebbles. There are other noisemaking customs. Oriental Jews write Haman's name on the soles of their shoes and stamp on it. Others knock stones together, or use trumpets, drums, hammers, or hand-clapping to make noise.

There are many reasons given for Mordechai's refusal to bow down to Haman. The popular interpretation is that a Jew bows only to God. But Jews were known to bow down to kings and high officials, and the text seems to indicate only Mordechai, among the Jews of Shushan, refused. Another suggestion is that Haman was descended from the wicked Amalekites, and Mordechai would not bow down to an enemy of the Jews. Still others say Haman wore an icon on his chest and Mordechai refused to worship idols. Rashi, the great commentator, explained that Mordechai would not bow down because Haman claimed to be divine.

If you lived in Shushan, would you have bowed down to Haman? Would you have been scared of him, even a little?

Have you ever been in a situation where you alone took an unpopular postion? What difficulties did this cause you?

Anti-Semites have long accused Jews of not being loyal citizens. *Give other examples from history and current events.*

Purim's name comes from the verse where Haman draws lots (*purim* in Hebrew) to determine the day the Jews would be destroyed. Some compare casting *purim* to tossing special sticks or coins in a fortune telling ritual, such as the I Ching.

Mordechai and Vashti both refused unreasonable demands. Vashti refused to appear at Ahashuerus's party, and Mordechai refused to bow down to Haman. Vashti was condemned, and Mordechai was praised.

How do you explain this?

Some call Purim the "holiday of the diaspora." What risks do the Jewish people assume living in the diaspora? What different problems do they face living as a majority in the land of Israel?

Why do you think it was so easy for Haman to persuade Ahashuerus that the Jews were a threat? Did his offer of money have anything to do with it?

Why doesn't Ahashuerus even make the effort to investigate Haman's charges?

Haman's anger against Mordechai was so great that he was willing to eliminate an entire people because of it.

Can you describe a situation where someone's anger got out of control?

ANI PURIM

Folk Song

A - ni Pu - rim a - ni Pu - rim sa - me - ach um - va - de - ach ha -

lo rak pa - am ba - sha - na a - vo l'-hit - a - re - ach la la la la la la la

la la la la la la la la la la la la la la

2.

Heydad Purim, heydad Purim
Haku tof um 'tziltayim
Hoy mi yiten uva Purim
Lechodesh lechodshayim.

3.

Rabi Purim, rabi Purim
Emor na li madua
Madua lo yachal Purim
Pa amayim bashavua.

1.

My name is Purim and I come
Great fun and frolic bringing,
Just once a year I visit you
To cheer you with my singing.
La, la, la, la, la, etc.

2.

Hurrah Purim! Hurrah Purim!
I love your merry drumming
And if I had my way, Purim,
Each month you would be coming.
La, la, la, la, la, etc.

Oh, Mr. Purim tell us why
We see you only yearly?
Please make it once or twice a week
Because we love you dearly.
La, la, la, la, la, la, la, etc.

וּמָרְדֳּכַי יָדַע אֶת־כָּל־אֲשֶׁר נַעֲשָׂה וַיִּקְרַע מָרְדֳּכַי אֶת־בְּגָדָיו וַיִּלְבַּשׁ שַׂק וָאֵפֶר וַיֵּצֵא בְּתוֹךְ הָעִיר וַיִּזְעַק זְעָקָה גְדוֹלָה וּמָרָה: וַיָּבוֹא עַד לִפְנֵי שַׁעַר־הַמֶּלֶךְ כִּי אֵין לָבוֹא אֶל־שַׁעַר הַמֶּלֶךְ בִּלְבוּשׁ שָׂק: וּבְכָל־ מְדִינָה וּמְדִינָה מְקוֹם אֲשֶׁר דְּבַר־הַמֶּלֶךְ וְדָתוֹ מַגִּיעַ אֵבֶל גָּדוֹל לַיְּהוּדִים וְצוֹם וּבְכִי וּמִסְפֵּד שַׂק וָאֵפֶר יֻצַּע לָרַבִּים:

In every province of the land, Jews could be found fasting, weeping and wailing. Mordechai tore his clothes and put on sack cloth. Esther sent him a message asking about the cause of this great mourning. Mordechai sent back word of the King's decree and begged Esther to go to Ahashuerus and plead for her people. But Esther was afraid. "Everyone at the court knows that it is forbidden to enter the King's presence without being summoned," she responded. "I could be put to death if I appear before him."

Mordechai replied, "You are also a Jew. Do not assume that you alone will escape our terrible fate. If you keep silent, you will surely die. Perhaps you have become Queen for just such a crisis."

Esther agreed to risk her life to save her people. "Tell all the Jews of Persia to fast for me for three days. I, too, will fast. At the end of the three days, I shall go to the King. If I am to perish, I shall perish." So Mordechai did as Esther commanded him.

There is no mention of prayer in the Purim story. The Jews did not pray when they heard the King's decree. Esther fasted, but did not pray as she prepared to approach the King. Nor is there mention of prayers of Thanksgiving after the victory. Some say that the Purim story was more likely a carnival tale than a historical account, and that Purim, like Mardi Gras, was a festival rite of spring. In this context it would be inappropriate to invoke the name of God.

Do you think that the Purim story actually happened? Does it matter?

Was it mazal (luck) that Esther was "in the right place at the right time," or was it an act of God? Does your answer make a difference in how you think about the story?

Is Esther any less a heroine because she was initially reluctant to save her people, or was she especially brave to overcome her fear?

✽✽✽✽✽✽✽✽✽✽✽✽✽✽

Was it fair for Mordechai to ask Esther to risk her life?
Who in modern times has risked his/her life for others?

Why do you think Esther did not know of the edict against the Jews until Mordechai sent her a message? Was she isolated, or was she just indifferent to their situation?

✽✽✽✽✽✽✽✽✽✽✽✽✽✽

The day before Purim is called "Ta'anit Esther", the Fast of Esther. Some people fast on this day to remember that for three days Queen Esther did not eat or sleep while she gathered courage to help her save the Jewish people.

וַיְהִי בַּיּוֹם הַשְּׁלִישִׁי וַתִּלְבַּשׁ אֶסְתֵּר
מַלְכוּת וַתַּעֲמֹד בַּחֲצַר בֵּית־הַמֶּלֶךְ
הַפְּנִימִית נֹכַח בֵּית הַמֶּלֶךְ וְהַמֶּלֶךְ יוֹשֵׁב
עַל־כִּסֵּא מַלְכוּתוֹ בְּבֵית הַמַּלְכוּת נֹכַח
פֶּתַח הַבָּיִת: וַיְהִי כִרְאוֹת הַמֶּלֶךְ אֶת־
אֶסְתֵּר הַמַּלְכָּה עֹמֶדֶת בֶּחָצֵר נָשְׂאָה חֵן
בְּעֵינָיו וַיּוֹשֶׁט הַמֶּלֶךְ לְאֶסְתֵּר אֶת־
שַׁרְבִיט הַזָּהָב אֲשֶׁר בְּיָדוֹ וַתִּקְרַב אֶסְתֵּר
וַתִּגַּע בְּרֹאשׁ הַשַּׁרְבִיט: וַיֹּאמֶר לָהּ הַמֶּלֶךְ
מַה־לָּךְ אֶסְתֵּר הַמַּלְכָּה וּמַה־בַּקָּשָׁתֵךְ
עַד־חֲצִי הַמַּלְכוּת וְיִנָּתֵן לָךְ:

On the third day, Esther put on her royal robes and came before the King. As soon as Ahashuerus saw her, he held out his golden scepter and asked, "What troubles you and what is your request? I am ready to grant you half my kingdom." "If it pleases Your Majesty," Esther replied, "I would like to invite you and HAMAN to a feast that I have prepared." The king quickly accepted her invitation.

At the feast, Ahashuerus again offered Esther whatever her heart desired. She asked only that he and HAMAN return for another party.

HAMAN left feeling cheerful, but soon his mood was spoiled. Mordechai stood at the palace gate and once again did not rise to honor him. HAMAN confided to his wife Zeresh and his closest friends, "I cannot enjoy all the good fortune that has come to me, because of Mordechai the Jew." "Let a gallows be put up," they suggested, "and ask the King to hang Mordechai on it. Then you can go happily to Esther's feast and enjoy yourself." This idea pleased HAMAN, and he had the gallows built.

When Vashti refused to listen to Ahashuerus, he became angry. When Esther approached the King without permission, he showed mercy.
Why do you think this was so?

Esther uses her charm and her beauty to save her people.
What do you think of Esther as a role model?

Esther rejects Ahashuerus' offer of "half the kingdom" for herself. Instead, she seeks security for her people. Because of this noble act, she is always remembered and loved.

What might have happened if the king had been so angry when Esther came before him, that he had banished her?
What other "what if's" can you think of that would have changed the Purim story?

The Midrash says that anyone to whom a miracle happens may establish a local Purim to celebrate. Many communities have celebrated the anniversaries of their victories over such dangers as riots, fire, and anti-Semitic pogroms. Some examples are:

Powder Purim: In 1804, Abraham Danzig of Vilna and his family were saved from dying in a gunpowder explosion.

French Purim: In the 18th century, during the Napoleonic wars, the Jews were terrorized and the synogogue invaded. The French soldiers saved the community.

Damascus Purim: In 1743, the governor of Damascus besieged Tiberias. The Jews suffered for 83 days until the siege was lifted, and the Jews were saved.

בַּלַּיְלָה הַהוּא נָדְדָה שְׁנַת הַמֶּלֶךְ וַיֹּאמֶר
לְהָבִיא אֶת־סֵפֶר הַזִּכְרֹנוֹת דִּבְרֵי הַיָּמִים
וַיִּהְיוּ נִקְרָאִים לִפְנֵי הַמֶּלֶךְ: וַיִּמָּצֵא כָתוּב
אֲשֶׁר הִגִּיד מָרְדֳּכַי עַל־בִּגְתָנָא וָתֶרֶשׁ שְׁנֵי
סָרִיסֵי הַמֶּלֶךְ מִשֹּׁמְרֵי הַסַּף אֲשֶׁר בִּקְשׁוּ
לִשְׁלֹחַ יָד בַּמֶּלֶךְ אֲחַשְׁוֵרוֹשׁ: וַיֹּאמֶר
הַמֶּלֶךְ מַה־נַּעֲשָׂה יְקָר וּגְדוּלָּה לְמָרְדֳּכַי
עַל־זֶה וַיֹּאמְרוּ נַעֲרֵי הַמֶּלֶךְ מְשָׁרְתָיו לֹא־
נַעֲשָׂה עִמּוֹ דָּבָר:

That night King Ahashuerus could not sleep. To pass the time, he had his record book brought to him. He read of the time Mordechai had saved his life by revealing the plot of Bigthan and Teresh. "What honor did I give Mordechai for this?" he asked. "Nothing has been done for him," his servants replied.

Just then, HAMAN came to speak to the King about hanging Mordechai. But before HAMAN could present his evil plan, Ahashuerus asked him to suggest a way to honor someone who pleases the King. Thinking that the King meant to honor him, HAMAN proposed that the man be dressed in palace robes and given the finest royal horse. He should be led through the city square while someone announces, "This is being done for a man the King wishes to honor!"

"Quick," Ahashuerus ordered HAMAN. "Do this for Mordechai!"

In disbelief, HAMAN did as the King commanded.

Masquerades and Purim plays *(shpiels)* have been a tradition for several hundred years. Actors dress in funny costumes and make fun of Bible stories, synagogue prayers, and rabbis' sermons. Some think these customs are adaptations of the spring Mardi Gras festival. In Israel's cities today, huge parades take place, called *Adloyada,* which in Hebrew means "until you don't know." This refers to the tradition that on Purim people should drink until they can no longer tell the difference between the phrases "Cursed be Haman" and "Blessed be Mordechai."

The scene of Haman leading Mordechai through town on horseback, dressed in the King's robes is considered to be the first Purim shpiel.

Why do you think so?

Who today deserves honor, and how would you honor them?

Imagine how Haman felt when he had to lead Mordechai through town on the King's best horse!

Did you ever have to be especially nice to someone you didn't like? What happened? How did you feel?

When we think of the Megillah, we usually think of the Purim Megillah or the *Book of Esther,* but there are actually five books of the Bible known as the Megillot. Each of them is read on a different holiday:

The Book of Esther — Purim
The Book of Ruth — Shavuot
Song of Songs — Pesach
Ecclesiastes — Sukkot
Lamentations — Tisha B'Av

וַיָּבֹא הַמֶּלֶךְ וְהָמָן לִשְׁתּוֹת עִם־אֶסְתֵּר הַמַּלְכָּה: וַיֹּאמֶר הַמֶּלֶךְ לְאֶסְתֵּר גַּם בַּיּוֹם הַשֵּׁנִי בְּמִשְׁתֵּה הַיַּיִן מַה־שְּׁאֵלָתֵךְ אֶסְתֵּר הַמַּלְכָּה וְתִנָּתֵן לָךְ וּמַה־בַּקָּשָׁתֵךְ עַד־חֲצִי הַמַּלְכוּת וְתֵעָשׂ: וַתַּעַן אֶסְתֵּר הַמַּלְכָּה וַתֹּאמַר אִם־מָצָאתִי חֵן בְּעֵינֶיךָ הַמֶּלֶךְ וְאִם־עַל־הַמֶּלֶךְ טוֹב תִּנָּתֶן לִי נַפְשִׁי בִּשְׁאֵלָתִי וְעַמִּי בְּבַקָּשָׁתִי:

The King and HAMAN came to the second feast. Again, Ahashuerus asked Esther what she desired. "I am ready to grant you half my kingdom," he stated. Esther pleaded, "Let my life be granted as well as my people's, for they are condemned to die by the hand of a great enemy." The King asked her to name the great enemy. "Your Majesty, it is none other than HAMAN!" she answered. Furious, the King ordered his servants to end HAMAN's life on the very gallows that HAMAN had built for Mordechai.

Why does Ahashuerus seem not to know who the enemy of Esther's people is? Didn't he approve Haman's plan?

❋❋❋❋❋❋❋❋❋❋❋❋❋❋❋

Banquets play a major role in the Purim story.
How are banquets and parties used to influence people today?

Why do you think Esther invited the King and Haman to two feasts?

❋❋❋❋❋❋❋❋❋❋❋❋❋❋❋

Food is an important part of Jewish celebration. When one thinks of Purim, the hamantaschen comes to mind; latkes are the food of Hanukkah. The Latke-Hamantasch Debate was created almost 50 years ago as a Purim program at the B'nai B'rith Hillel Foundation at the University of Chicago. Now an annual event at many universities, it features academics from all fields debating the relative merits of these holiday treats. Recent papers have analyzed these foods from sociological, legal, artistic, nutritional, and economic perspectives.

Which is your favorite and why?

❋❋❋❋❋❋❋❋❋❋❋❋❋❋❋

At the beginning of the story, Ahashuerus refuses to honor Vashti's wishes. At the end, he listens to Esther.

Has he learned anything?

❋❋❋❋❋❋❋❋❋❋❋❋❋❋❋

Why do you think the Megillah is called The Book of Esther *and not* The Book of Esther and Mordechai?

בַּיּוֹם הַהוּא נָתַן הַמֶּלֶךְ אֲחַשְׁוֵרוֹשׁ
לְאֶסְתֵּר הַמַּלְכָּה אֶת־בֵּית הָמָן צֹרֵר
הַיְּהוּדִים וּמָרְדֳּכַי בָּא לִפְנֵי הַמֶּלֶךְ כִּי־
הִגִּידָה אֶסְתֵּר מָה הוּא־לָהּ: וַיָּסַר הַמֶּלֶךְ
אֶת־טַבַּעְתּוֹ אֲשֶׁר הֶעֱבִיר מֵהָמָן וַיִּתְּנָהּ
לְמָרְדֳּכָי וַתָּשֶׂם אֶסְתֵּר אֶת־מָרְדֳּכַי עַל־
בֵּית הָמָן: וַתּוֹסֶף אֶסְתֵּר וַתְּדַבֵּר לִפְנֵי
הַמֶּלֶךְ וַתִּפֹּל לִפְנֵי רַגְלָיו וַתֵּבְךְּ וַתִּתְחַנֶּן־
לוֹ לְהַעֲבִיר אֶת־רָעַת הָמָן הָאֲגָגִי וְאֵת
מַחֲשַׁבְתּוֹ אֲשֶׁר חָשַׁב עַל־הַיְּהוּדִים:

The King gave Esther HAMAN's estate, and Mordechai was put in a position of power. Esther begged the King to stop the edict to destroy the Jews on the 13th of Adar. "How can I bear to see the disaster which will befall my people!" she cried. The King explained that he could not revoke a royal decree, but he told Mordechai to issue a new decree. So Mordechai wrote in the name of the King that on the 13th of Adar, the Jews were permitted to fight back and destroy all who might attack them, and could take their possessions. Couriers on horseback carried the news throughout the land. There was gladness and joy among the Jews.

Why do you think the King could not revoke a royal decree?

Could he or anyone else have made a plea for a non-violent solution to the problem?

The Purim story has all the ingredients of a gripping drama—suspense, love, and violence. It is often compared to another exciting Biblical story, that of Joseph. Pharaoh's dream of the seven fat and lean cows is compared to King Ahashuerus' inability to sleep. Two of Pharaoh's ministers offended him; two of Ahasuerus' plotted to kill him. Pharaoh took off his signet ring and put it upon Joseph's hand; the King removed his ring and gave it to Haman (and later to Mordechai). Both Joseph and Mordechai were paraded before the people to receive their honor, and both dressed in royal robes after they were appointed to high office.

Can you find other similarities?

The longest sentence in the Bible is in this chapter. Verse 9 has 43 words in Hebrew and about double that number in English.

וּבִשְׁנֵים֩ עָשָׂ֨ר חֹ֜דֶשׁ הוּא־חֹ֣דֶשׁ אֲדָ֗ר
בִּשְׁלוֹשָׁ֨ה עָשָׂ֥ר יוֹם֙ בּ֔וֹ אֲשֶׁ֨ר הִגִּ֧יעַ דְּבַר־
הַמֶּ֛לֶךְ וְדָת֖וֹ לְהֵעָשׂ֑וֹת בַּיּ֗וֹם אֲשֶׁ֨ר שִׂבְּר֜וּ
אֹיְבֵ֤י הַיְּהוּדִים֙ לִשְׁל֣וֹט בָּהֶ֔ם וְנַהֲפ֣וֹךְ ה֔וּא
אֲשֶׁ֨ר יִשְׁלְט֧וּ הַיְּהוּדִ֛ים הֵ֖מָּה בְּשֹׂנְאֵיהֶֽם׃
נִקְהֲל֨וּ הַיְּהוּדִ֜ים בְּעָרֵיהֶ֗ם בְּכָל־מְדִינוֹת֙
הַמֶּ֣לֶךְ אֲחַשְׁוֵר֔וֹשׁ לִשְׁלֹ֣חַ יָ֔ד בִּמְבַקְשֵׁ֖י
רָֽעָתָ֑ם וְאִישׁ֙ לֹא־עָמַ֣ד בִּפְנֵיהֶ֔ם כִּֽי־נָפַ֥ל
פַּחְדָּ֖ם   עַל־כָּל־הָֽעַמִּֽים׃

And so, on the 13th day of Adar, the Jews were victorious. Many Persians were slain in Shushan and in the provinces throughout the kingdom. Included were the ten sons of HAMAN (Parshandatha, Dalphon, Aspatha, Poratha, Adalia, Aridatha, Parmastha, Arisai, Aridai and Vaizatha). Although permitted by the King's order, the Jews did not take any of their victims' possessions or property.

Mordechai and Esther proclaimed that the Jews of Persia should observe the 14th and 15th days of Adar every year to remember how their mourning and grief had been turned to feasting and gladness. It would be an occasion for sending gifts to one another and giving charity to the poor.

They agreed that these days of Purim would always be remembered among the Jews and their descendants.

It is customary to quickly read the names of Haman's sons in one breath to teach us not to rejoice in the downfall of our enemies.

If one interprets the Purim story as fiction, this chapter is the ultimate fantasy. The Jews, who normally are the victims, reverse roles with their enemies. In times when Jews were persecuted, it was a story of hope. On the other hand, it raises questions about how Jews should act when they have power.

Chapter IX is the basis for the customs of the holiday: a festive meal, the exchange of gifts, and giving charity to the poor.

There are seven mitzvot of Purim:

1. Reading the Megillah
2. Sending *shalach manot* (packages of food) to friends and family
3. Giving gifts to the poor
4. Reading a special Torah portion
5. Adding the reading "For the Miracles" to daily prayers
6. Making a Purim *seudah* or feast
7. Refraining from fasting and giving eulogies

The fourth stanza of *Rock of Ages,* the song traditionally sung after lighting the Hanukkah candles, praises God for the deliverance of Israel from Haman's plot.

וַיָּשֶׂם הַמֶּלֶךְ אֲחַשְׁוֵרֹשׁ מַס עַל־הָאָרֶץ
וְאִיֵּי הַיָּם: וְכָל־מַעֲשֵׂה תָקְפּוֹ וּגְבוּרָתוֹ
וּפָרָשַׁת גְּדֻלַּת מָרְדֳּכַי אֲשֶׁר גִּדְּלוֹ הַמֶּלֶךְ
הֲלוֹא־הֵם כְּתוּבִים עַל־סֵפֶר דִּבְרֵי הַיָּמִים
לְמַלְכֵי מָדַי וּפָרָס: כִּי מָרְדֳּכַי הַיְּהוּדִי
מִשְׁנֶה לַמֶּלֶךְ אֲחַשְׁוֵרוֹשׁ וְגָדוֹל לַיְּהוּדִים
וְרָצוּי לְרֹב אֶחָיו דֹּרֵשׁ טוֹב לְעַמּוֹ וְדֹבֵר
שָׁלוֹם לְכָל־זַרְעוֹ:

Ahashuerus appointed Mordechai to be second in command in all of Persia. Mordechai was highly regarded by
the Jews for he continually looked after their welfare.

AFTER READING THE MEGILLAH WE SAY:

בָּרוּךְ אַתָּה, יְיָ אֱלֹהֵינוּ, מֶלֶךְ הָעוֹלָם, הָרָב אֶת רִיבֵנוּ וְהַדָּן
אֶת דִּינֵנוּ וְהַנּוֹקֵם אֶת נִקְמָתֵנוּ וְהַנִּפְרָע לָנוּ מִצָּרֵינוּ וְהַמְשַׁלֵּם
גְּמוּל לְכָל אֹיְבֵי נַפְשֵׁנוּ. בָּרוּךְ אַתָּה, יְיָ, הַנִּפְרָע לְעַמּוֹ יִשְׂרָאֵל
מִכָּל צָרֵיהֶם הָאֵל הַמּוֹשִׁיעַ.

Baruch Atah Adonai Eloheinu melech ha'olam. Harav et rivenu.
V'hadan et dinenu. V'hanokem et nikmatenu. V'hanifra lanu
mitzareinu. V'ham'shalem g'mul l'chal oyvei nafshenu. Baruch
Atah Adonai hanifra l'amo Yisrael mikal tzareihem. Ha'el
hamoshia.

We praise You, Adonai our God, Ruler of the Universe, Who
upholds our cause, defends us, and brings punishment upon
our enemies. We praise You, Adonai, Protector of Israel.

Yom Kippur, the Day of Atonement, is also referred to in the plural, *Yom Kippurim.* This can also be read as *Yom Ke-Purim,* a day like Purim. On both days our lot is cast, and things are topsy-turvy.

What is topsy-turvy about Yom Kippur? What is topsy-turvy about Purim?

Mordechai continues to be loyal to his people.

Do you feel one can be a politician or business leader and remain a good Jew?

The name of God is not mentioned in the Purim story. Some say this teaches us that God only seems concealed from us. Others say it emphasizes that people must show courage, sacrifice and heroism to bring about their own redemption. Because the name of God never appears, the Purim Megillah was often illustrated and illuminated.

Does Purim have special meaning after the Holocaust?

The Midrash says that in the Messianic age, all other festivals will be abolished, but Purim will remain.

Why do you think this is so?

THE PURIM STORY
A PLAY IN TEN SCENES

Production notes

For younger children especially, the Megillah may be done as a play or dramatic reading. It would work equally well with adults or children taking the parts. Costumes or masks are highly recommended. You may use scenery or just simple props.

Invite the audience to participate, cheering Mordechai as he enters, booing Haman and whirling groggers after he speaks.

Make decorative programs in the form of miniature scrolls.

Characters

This text has been written for the following 18 characters:

Narrator	*Mordechai*	*4 queen contestants*
Ahashuerus	*Zeresh*	*Messenger*
Haman	*4 nobles*	*Horse*
Esther	*2 advisors*	

If fewer cast members are available, parts may be combined. If you want more children to participate, the narrator part may be divided up, and nobles, advisors, and contestants may be added.

Setting

King Ahashuerus's Court in Shushan, Persia, 5th century BCE. The stage may be divided into the King's room, the Queen's room, Haman's house, and the palace courtyard. (See diagram.)

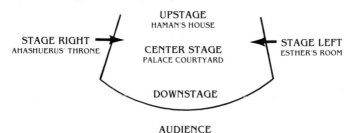

Props

Proclamation scroll for noble
Thrones and crowns for Ahashuerus and Esther
A table and three chairs in Esther's room
A wine or soda bottle and cup for the king
A scepter for Ahashuerus
A few dishes for Esther's banquet

More props and scenery, including murals and backdrop decorations, would be welcome. Costumes may be more elaborate.

SCENE I

Characters: *Narrator, Ahashuerus, two nobles, two advisors, messenger.*

Setting: *The king's room. Ahashuerus is seated on his throne, drinking. His nobles and advisors attend him. The narrator enters.*

Narrator: Our Purim tale begins in the palace of Ahashuerus, ruler of Persia.

Ahashuerus: Nobles and loyal subjects, welcome to another day of feasting and merrymaking.

Noble 1: All hail Ahashuerus, ruler of 127 provinces from India to Ethiopia! *(All cheer.)*

Noble 2 *(aside):* And champion guzzler of spirits!

Ahashuerus *(claps, summoning messenger):* Go to Vashti, my queen. She is in her palace giving a feast for the women. Order her to appear before us so that we might admire her beauty.

Messenger: But, Your Majesty, it is not customary for the queen to be present once the drinking has begun. It is not right!

Ahashuerus: Silence! My orders are to be obeyed.

(Messenger leaves and returns alone.)

Messenger: My Lord, she has refused to appear.

Ahashuerus: My queen dares to disobey my orders? Advisors, quickly, tell me what I should do.

Advisor 1 *(leans in on one side of Ahashuerus):* Vashti has offended Your Majesty.

Advisor 2 *(leans in on the other side of Ahashuerus):* She should be banished from the throne.

Ahashuerus: So be it!

(Messenger and nobles exit. Narrator enters.)

Narrator: Time passes and Ahashuerus misses Queen Vashti. Perhaps he should have admired her good qualities instead of being so quick to criticize. *(Exits.)*

Ahashuerus *(to advisors):* Woe is me. With Vashti gone, I'm unbearably lonely. Now what should I do?

Advisor 2 *(leaning in again):* The solution is obvious. We must replace her.

Advisor 1 *(leaning in on the other side):* We will organize a beauty contest and send word throughout the land. Every maiden shall participate.

Ahashuerus: So be it!

SCENE II

Characters: *Narrator, king, two nobles, two advisors, four contestants, Esther, Mordechai.*

Setting: *The courtyard. The king, his nobles and advisors, stand to one side, while four contestants cross the stage performing in turn. One may dance, one may sing, one may twirl a baton, one may do cartwheels, etc. Musical accompaniment is optional.*
As the narrator begins to speak, Esther enters and walks simply across the stage. The king points to her, and one of his nobles crowns her. Nobles and advisors exit. King takes his place on his throne.

Narrator: Although many beautiful young women appeared before the king, only Esther won his heart. Let's listen as the new queen talks to her cousin and guardian, Mordechai... *(Exits.)*

Mordechai *(enters and joins Esther)*: My dear Esther, it is still hard to believe that you, a Jewish maiden, have been crowned Queen of Persia. May your luck and fortune continue.

Esther: Thank you, cousin Mordechai. Please know that I have followed your advice and have not revealed my family or my people to the king.

Mordechai: Good! But here's something you can reveal. I overheard two of the king's servants, Bigtan and Teresh, plotting to kill him. You must report this to Ahashuerus.

Esther: I will. I'm sure he will punish them, and then write all about it in his record book. *(Mordechai exits. Esther crosses stage and takes her seat on her throne.)*

SCENE III

Characters: *Narrator, Haman, four nobles, two advisors, Mordechai.*

Setting: *The courtyard. Narrator enters.*

Narrator *(like a TV announcer)*: Will Esther and her king live happily ever after? Or is there trouble on the horizon? We will soon learn the answer, because a nobleman is about to make a proclamation. *(Exits.)*

(Nobles and advisors enter. Noble 3 carries a large vertical scroll.)

Noble 3 *(reading)*: Here ye, inhabitants of the king's court. King Ahashuerus has promoted HAMAN to be his Prime Minister.

Haman *(enters upstage and struts downstage toward nobles):* I am now your lord and ruler. Everyone will bow down to me when I pass by.

As Haman passes nobles and advisors, each one in turn bows down...and remains bowed. Mordechai enters. Haman walks in front of him, but Mordechai remains standing.

Noble 4 *(looks up):* Mordechai, why are you not bowing before HAMAN?

Mordechai: As a Jew, I cannot bow down to a descendant of Agog, the cruel Amalakite king. And most important, I pledge my allegiance to the One God who is the true Ruler of the Universe.

Haman: I will have my revenge! *(Haman and nobles exit right; Mordechai exits left.)*

SCENE IV

Characters: *Ahashuerus, Narrator, Haman, two nobles.*

Setting: *Ahashuerus's room. Ahashuerus is seated on his throne. Two nobles guard him. Narrator enters.*

Narrator: To achieve his goal HAMAN needs the help of Ahashuerus, the king. *(Exits.)*

Haman *(enters):* Your Royal Highness, my Lord and Ruler. May I have your ear?

Ahashuerus: Speak, my loyal Prime Minister.

Haman: There is a certain people, scattered and dispersed throughout your kingdom, whose laws are different from ours. These people do not obey our laws. They are not loyal subjects. I advise that an edict be drawn for their destruction.

Ahashuerus: Must such a drastic measure be taken, HAMAN?

Haman: . . .And I will pay 10,000 talents of silver to your royal treasury.

Ahashuerus *(smiling):* Well, perhaps we should proceed with your plan. When will it occur?

Haman: I have cast lots — Purim — and have determined that the 13th day of the month of Adar should be the designated time.

Ahashuerus: So be it. *(Haman and nobles exit; Ahashuerus remains seated.)*

SCENE V

Characters: *Narrator, Esther, Messenger.*

Setting: *Esther's room. Narrator enters.*

Narrator: Esther has learned that the Jews outside the palace are acting as if they are in mourning. They have put on sackcloth and rubbed ashes on themselves. They are weeping and wailing. She has sent a messenger to Mordechai for an explanation. *(Exits.)*

(Messenger enters.)

Esther: What news do you bring?

Messenger: Your cousin Mordechai reports that the Jewish people are in great danger. HAMAN has obtained a royal edict to destroy the Jews on the 13th of Adar. Mordechai begs you to go before the king to plead the cause of the Jews.

Esther: How can I go before the king without being summoned? It is forbidden. I could lose my life!

Messenger: Your cousin Mordechai says you must risk your life to save your people. If you don't, your life, too, may not be spared. He thinks perhaps you have attained your royal position for just such a crisis.

Esther: You are right. Tell all the Jews to fast for me for three days. I too will fast. Then I shall go the the king. *(Esther and messenger exit.)*

SCENE VI

Characters: *Narrator, Ahashuerus, Esther.*

Setting: *King's room. Narrator enters. While he is speaking, Esther enters, newly attired, and crosses to king's room.*

Narrator: Following her three-day fast, Esther puts on her royal attire and comes before the king. As soon as Ahashuerus sees her, she wins his favor and he extends his scepter to her. *(Exits.)*

Ahashuerus *(extends scepter, then takes Esther's hand):* Esther, my lovely queen, what is troubling you? I am prepared to give you anything you wish — to half my kingdom.

Esther: I have come to invite you to a feast I have prepared. And I want you to bring HAMAN.

Ahashuerus: We will accept with pleasure! *(King remains seated. Esther returns to her throne.)*

SCENE VII

Characters: *Haman, Zeresh, Mordechai, Narrator.*

Setting: *Courtyard, then Haman's house. Narrator and Mordechai enter right. When Haman enters left, Mordechai refuses to bow down. Haman turns his back in anger and crosses upstage to his house where Zeresh awaits him. Mordechai exits.*

Narrator: HAMAN leaves the palace and happens to pass Mordechai, who does not bow down to him. When HAMAN arrives home, he angrily reports this to Zeresh. *(Exits.)*

Haman: Zeresh, my anger knows no bounds! That arrogant Jew, Mordechai, still will not bow to me.

Zeresh: Enough is enough, HAMAN. Prepare a gallows to hang him.

Haman: My dear wife, I will follow your wise counsel. *(Haman and Zeresh exit.)*

SCENE VIII

Characters: *Narrator, Haman, Mordechai, horse.*

Setting: *Courtyard. Haman is leading Mordechai on a horse (a broom or another player). In the background, Esther is setting the table for the feast. Narrator enters.*

Narrator: We are witnessing an unbelievable sight. Mordechai, dressed in royal garb, and seated on the king's finest horse, is being led around the courtyard by none other than HAMAN.

Haman *(leading Mordechai):* This is done for the man the king wishes to honor. *(repeats over & over in grudging voice)*

Narrator: HAMAN, how did this happen? *(If Mordechai is riding a "person" horse, he may want to dismount to give the horse a rest.)*

Haman: Who would have imagined that when the king asked how to honor someone, he meant Mordechai the Jew and not me! How could I have known that Mordechai saved the king's life? It happened before I was Prime Minister.

Curse that night he couldn't sleep. He called for his record book and read how Mordechai saved him from Bigtan and Teresh's murderous plot. So Mordechai is rewarded, and I'm embarrassed, humiliated. I want revenge more than ever!

(Mordechai remounts, and Haman leads him off stage continuing to repeat, "This is done . . ." Haman re-enters and joins Ahashuerus at Esther's feast.)

SCENE IX

Characters: *Narrator, Esther, Haman, Ahashuerus.*

Setting: *Esther's room. All are seated at table. Narrator enters.*

Narrator: Does HAMAN fare better at Esther's feast? *(Exits.)*

Ahashuerus: Esther, my dear, this is such a sumptuous feast. Don't you agree, HAMAN?

Haman: Why, yes, it is especially tasty.

Ahashuerus: But Esther, why do you look so distressed? Is something troubling you?

Esther: Oh, Your Majesty, I, and my entire people, are scheduled to die at the hand of a dangerous enemy.

Ahashuerus: Who is this great enemy, my dear?

Esther: It is none other than HAMAN! *(Haman shrinks into background.)*

Ahashuerus: Can it be that my own prime minister has deceived me?

Esther: Indeed he has! You see, his pride is as big as your empire. And his compassion is as small as your ring.

Ahashuerus: Away with you, HAMAN. You shall perish on the same gallows that you built for Mordechai. *(Haman runs off.)* Esther, stay and tell me how this all happened.

Esther: I will Your Majesty, but first let us send couriers throughout the land to announce the good news. The Jews will be saved! *(All exit.)*

SCENE X

Characters: *Narrator, Esther, Mordechai.*

Setting: *Courtyard. Narrator enters.*

Narrator: Ahashuerus gave HAMAN's riches to Esther, and appointed Mordechai to a powerful position in his kingdom. Will success spoil our heroes?. The answer is clearly NO.

Esther *(enters)*: We have won out against our enemies. Now we must use our wealth and power for the good of our people.

Mordechai *(enters and joins Esther)*: Yes, and each year we must remember these days, when our mourning and grief turned to feasting and merrymaking.

Esther: Yes, it should be a time to celebrate, to give gifts to each other, and charity to the poor.

Mordechai: Let us call it the holiday of Purim. It will be a time of joy for the Jewish people in every generation.

(Players come on stage for a group bow.)